Unconditional Love Is…

Appreciating Aspects of Life

By

Harold W. Becker

White Fire Publishing

Unconditional Love Is...
Appreciating Aspects of Life

By Harold W. Becker

Copyright © 2010 Harold W. Becker

Published by:
White Fire Publishing
Tampa, Florida
www.whitefirepublishing.com

Cover Design and Interior Layout: John T. Goltz

Library of Congress Control Number: 2010929421

ISBN: 978-0-979046-02-5

First Printing: June 2010
Printed in the USA on acid free paper

The essence of life is found in the love that we share from our heart. Each of us walks the path of humanity on this planet and our laughter and our tears are universal. No one is ever truly alone.

Like a magnificent tapestry made of many colors and threads, the fabric of life connects each of us in wondrous ways. Whether we realize our impact or not we are forever affecting the world around us through our positive and less-than-positive expressions. By simply appreciating the many aspects of life that make us who we are, we begin to realize the truth of our unity.

As you weave your personal journey into this amazing adventure, you inspire others with your unconditional love.

Harold W. Becker

Unconditional Love Is...

Freedom
Peace
Wisdom
Life
Harmony
Joy
Compassion
Service
Dignity
Oneness
Purity
Hope
Charity
Liberty
Faith
Victory
Divinity
Kindness
Gratitude
Perfection
Beauty
Trust
Detachment
Forgiveness
New Beginnings
Concentration
Honesty
Justice
Integrity
Gentleness
Youth

Alertness
Inspiration
Guidance
Generosity
Activity
Understanding
Creativity
Imagination
Happiness
Purpose
Mastery
Grace
Abundance
Strength
Sincerity
Courage
Choice
Confidence
Health
Unity
Vitality
Power
Serenity
Courtesy
Success
Persistence
Achievement
Humility
Energy
Ability
Respect
Potential

Unconditional

Love

Is ...

Unconditional

Love

Is

Freedom

Freedom

Freedom is our eternal birthright. Each of us has within us the limitless potential to be whatever we choose. No person, place, condition, or thing can ever take it away; we can only give it away of our own volition. Yet, we must first acknowledge our freedom to make it real in our world.

To experience genuine freedom, we must give freedom. We can no longer expect others to do our will, nor can we continue to control or manipulate another. Instead, we can model the inner experience of freedom and radiate this for all to know. When we free ourselves of self-imposed limiting beliefs, we unlock our potential and become our dreams.

Unconditional love is freedom. Freely loving ourselves, those around us, and the rest of our world, allows us to express our true selves in the noblest way.

Unconditional

Love

Is

Peace

Peace

Peace is an inner quiet solitude which knows no bounds. It is like a clear mountain lake reflecting the highest peaks of wisdom. When we quiet the mind and feelings, we begin to experience the peace within that is always available. In this calm state we can contemplate the possibilities life affords and allow new inspiration for our journey.

Peace is not static, it is a dynamic and vibrant energy which permeates the depths of our existence and comforts us. The opportunity to realize our innate perfection resides in this stillness. When we tap into this amazing awareness, we know from whence truth comes and how to expand it. We recognize peace begins within and that we must consciously cultivate it to experience its gifts.

Unconditional love is peace. When we claim the serenity peace provides we find a vast reservoir of potential ideas, opportunities, and love.

Unconditional

Love

Is

Wisdom

Wisdom

Wisdom is born of the ages from inner thinking and contemplation. It is not to be confused with knowledge which gathers its information from outer sources. Wisdom is a silent reflection upon limitless ideas and the application of the highest possibility.

Wisdom is an expression of awareness derived from personal truth, experience and understanding. It acknowledges the balance of creation through love, wisdom, and power. To be wise is to know and practice truth of being, expanding every particle of life in the experience.

Unconditional love is wisdom. Wisdom is the truest sense of love since it recognizes potentiality and pursues it with a calm passion.

Unconditional

Love

Is

Life

Life

Our life is like a grand play that captures the momentary expressions of each of us. It is a never ending story of delights and challenges, joys and opportunities. As we imagine, write and perform in each act, we add our energy to the interplay and possibilities. The sum thus becomes more than the parts.

We are here to enjoy the experiences of our creation. Living life through love, we allow our choices to fulfill our dreams and to honor the dreams of others. Ever expanding in infinite ways, life calls to our hearts and guides us onward to evolve our potential and create more magnificent realities.

Unconditional love is Life. When we fill our days with joy and radiate our love to others, we experience a facet of life's potential.

Unconditional

Love

Is

Harmony

Harmony

To maintain harmony in our every thought and feeling is to experience the joy of unconditional love. It preserves and insures our balance and poise for right action. Each time we allow ourselves to drift from this central point, we touch the discord and challenge of mistaken awareness. Harmony is the beginning point of positive creation.

Finding balance in each moment is the sweetest key to every success. Knowing what is important and that which is not, leads us to a harmonious understanding and reverence for life itself. Nothing in life is worth disrupting our personal harmony and joyous expression. Sustaining harmony assures us of enjoying the process of living.

Unconditional love is harmony. No matter what is before you, seek harmony in the present moment and you will find infinite rewards of love to satisfy your effort.

Unconditional

Love

Is

Joy

Joy

Joy is the laughter of angels. This inner delight resonates and harmonizes all of our faculties and provides purpose to our adventure. It expands our heart and fills us with the energy to pursue our dreams. We naturally aspire to our preferences and no longer limit ourselves to just fulfilling our needs. Joy connects us to the divine angel in each of us.

We can choose a path of joy, making every decision based upon this inner prompting. It leads us with ease and grace, fulfilling our fondest wishes while ensuring our delight. Struggle and doubt cease as we allow joy into our daily expression. This magnificent quality of love reminds us of who and what we really are at heart.

Unconditional love is joy. Sing the song of joy and let each moment unfold its potential.

Unconditional

Love

Is

Compassion

Compassion

Compassion lifts the energy of any situation into its natural state of unconditional love. Unlike sympathy which believes in the mistake and empowers it, compassion conveys our warmth and respect along with strength, wisdom and understanding. It recognizes the divine perfection in every action and allows for this balance to return.

We have the power to lift the spirit of any person, place, or condition through our compassion. We begin with compassion for ourselves and our experiences. When we recognize the interconnection of all reality, we see the reflection in every experience and embrace the opportunity to raise the expression.

Unconditional love is compassion. Compassion shares the strength of love with everyone and everything.

Unconditional

Love

Is

Service

Service

Our daily activity is our service to humanity and the universe. No matter what we undertake in our routine or habits, we are engaging the energy of life. When we choose to use positive thoughts and feelings, we serve a greater purpose and expand the love around us. When we limit our expression through negativity and fear, we serve to ultimately destroy the good within and about us. It is always our choice whether we serve in love.

Every thought, feeling, and action provides an opportunity to assist in a higher capacity. Focusing on our service to life reminds us of our ability to use universal energy in constructive ways. When we view service as part of our life purpose, we no longer work at life. Instead, we enjoy the fruits of our labor.

Unconditional love is service. When we serve the cause of love, we ensure its abundant flow in our individual and collective experience.

Unconditional Love Is Dignity

Dignity

We come into this world filled with potential to create magnificent dreams. Our family, friends, community and culture all add their special gifts and together, we are here to share in this grand adventure. Each person embodies this inalienable and intrinsic right to explore their imagination and pursue their highest hopes for life.

Because we share this journey with others, we often depart from our own desires and lose sight of our deeper yearnings for life. We ignore our heart callings and in the process we misplace our self-respect. Our dignity is replaced with guilt and shame for perceived missed opportunities. By simply going within and trusting our heart, we reclaim our dignity.

Unconditional love is dignity. When we come from our own dignity, we embrace the grace and dignity of one another and encourage the highest and best for all.

Unconditional

Love

Is

Oneness

Oneness

Each cell works in harmony with the entire body just as our planet is in flawless alignment within our galaxy of galaxies. To understand this fantastic perfection of life is to know a oneness of exacting magnitude. Nothing is or ever will be out of place and each moment unfolds infinite riches in our experience.

The animal, plant, and mineral kingdoms respect this natural order and give of themselves to enhance this connection. We, in turn, have the same responsibility and opportunity to add our loving creation to this wondrous canvas. When we share in this evolving expression of beauty, we play our part within the whole.

Unconditional love is oneness. The rich tapestry of life weaves its love in every atom and allows us to play in the vast field of infinite oneness.

Unconditional

Love

Is

Purity

Purity

When we are pure of heart and mind we are free to express our unconditional love. The light of our being pours through us naturally and we share our happiness without condition or limitation. Purity is like a golden flame dissolving the old accumulation and revealing the perfection within each of us.

Extending the personal effort to clear away old emotional limitations and stifling thoughts provides terrific rewards. Every time we let go of negativity, fear, and doubt we purify our reality and enhance our potential through love. We literally expand our future of good in this process. Purity is a state of being that accepts the perfection already held within.

Unconditional love is purity. To know thyself and to desire purity is the way to reach for the stars and attain the dreams of love.

Unconditional

Love

Is

Hope

Hope

Life fills us with more than dreams made manifest. It surrounds us with the ever present hope that such wonders are possible. Hope paves the way to experiencing our potential. Through rhythmic actions of loving desire we steadily make our dreams real and it is the hope of possibility that sustains us through this process of manifestation.

At first we have hope a thing is possible. Eventually this hope becomes faith as we come to rely on its action. To lose hope however, is to lose faith in ourselves and only we can ever restore it. Through self love and trust in our abilities, we reclaim our internal power through the magical quality of hope which is our reminder in the potential of life itself.

Unconditional love is hope. When we have hope, we leave a space for the infinite power of love to rush in and immerse us in possibilities.

Unconditional

Love

Is

Charity

Charity

Charity begins with the self. As we go within and recognize our personal motivation and intent, we begin to realize our potential to love unconditionally. This inner awakening of self acceptance and understanding leads us to greater compassion for our self and others. Ignoring our innate needs depletes our willingness to give to others.

Taking the time to nurture ourselves allows us to tap the vast reservoir of our potential, encouraging us to give to others. Going within, we find that charity starts in our heart and radiates outward touching infinite lives with its wondrous light. Each act of self love becomes a selfless and charitable act for others.

Unconditional love is charity. There is a limitless supply of love available for everyone and charity provides the means of sharing it.

Unconditional
Love
Is
Liberty

Liberty

Everyone has the liberty to do as they please. Yet, each of us is also responsible for this immense freedom. What we take from another we take from ourselves. Similarly what we give out, we receive back in full measure. When we express our free will, we reap the consequences of our actions, be they good or not as good.

In the human kingdom there is such unbelievable potential to manifest exquisite beauty through love. Our infinite imagination is the source of our ability to choose the realities we wish to experience and claim our freedom. Through liberty we express our creative potential and share our bountiful gifts.

Unconditional love is liberty. We are at liberty to love each other through our thoughts, feelings, deeds and actions.

Unconditional

Love

Is

Faith

Faith

To believe in ourselves is to have faith in life. Ever surrounding us is the constant good life affords as proof of the possibilities. Without faith in ourselves, we often have little faith in life. We must learn to trust in our ability to create the lives we dream of.

When we seem to require it most, it is faith in our inner wisdom that carries us through. Having faith and trust in life at all times comes from knowing they are ever present and always available. Acknowledge your limitless potential and ability to rise above every situation through love. Faith - such a simple word with such enormous power.

Unconditional love is faith. To love life unconditionally is to have faith in that same life.

Unconditional

Love

Is

Victory

Victory

Moment to moment we choose our reality and therefore our victory - for every choice leads to another manifestation of creative thought. When we place our attention on positive goals and ideals, we cause our energy to focus upon these results. As sure as we do this, we reach our victorious completion and ready ourselves for the next experience.

Knowing our ability to create our world, we must acknowledge the victory inherent in its fulfillment. Such awareness allows us to confidently go forth with our innermost loving desires to create our ultimate dreams. When we accept our victory in the beginning, it will surely be there in the end.

Unconditional love is victory. A life lived in unconditional love is a life filled with victorious accomplishment.

Unconditional Love Is Divinity

Divinity

We are spiritual beings having a human experience. To recognize the sublime nature and potential within us is to realize our divinity. Given the power to love unconditionally, we can choose to use it every moment. We are truly angels at heart and delight in the journey of love.

Allowing the wisdom of our own higher self to guide us in our adventure of life is to share in the love that is ever present in our hearts. We have everything we require and desire inside us. Instead of seeking that which is without, we can use our energy to cultivate the potential we have within.

Unconditional love is divinity. Living life through love is being the divine angels we already are.

Unconditional

Love

Is

Kindness

Kindness

An expression of kindness can heal the hardest heart and repair the emotional pain of ages. Such acts born of simple dignity, allow the giver to share in the delight of unconditional love while the recipient is held in a state of grace. Nobler a deed is never done than through kindness.

Kindness generates a vibration flowing in ever spiraling waves touching many more than we ever realize. To be kind is to be gentle in spirit and countenance. These are the virtues to cultivate for real accomplishment.

Unconditional love is kindness. When we are kind to ourselves and one another, we create a part of heaven here on earth.

Unconditional

Love

Is

Gratitude

Gratitude

There is enormous power associated with gratitude. When we are grateful for the many things around us and the experiences we are entertaining in the moment, we expand the good in our lives. This conscious effort to notice every part of our reality helps us see our connection to all life.

From the simple and mundane to the trying, challenging and thrilling experiences, it is essential to gratefully acknowledge each for their expression. Everything and everyone in our path are there to help us become more of our potential; that is their gift. Be open to each moment and appreciate life.

Unconditional love is gratitude. Every particle of this physical reality shares itself with us for our enjoyment and growth. Gratitude is our opportunity to acknowledge and enjoy the experience.

Unconditional

Love

Is

Perfection

Perfection

Within the heart of each of us is a blueprint of perfection. From the original cell to the subsequent form we occupy, this image of perfection awaits in our consciousness to reveal our potential. By choosing unconditionally loving thoughts and feelings we come ever closer to this wondrous expression.

The human personality frequently scorns perfection as unattainable. Yet, as simply as we breathe, we can share our unconditional love and become the very nature of this perfection. At the center of every creation is the example of perfection waiting to manifest.

Unconditional love is perfection. In truth, we never leave the state of perfection except in our minds and feelings, for all things exist in this state naturally.

Unconditional

Love

Is

Beauty

Beauty

There is beauty within all creation. It is more than just physical; real beauty transcends all dimensions and emanates from the spirit within all things. It is the genuine expression in each of us. The presence of love reveals this truth every time we focus our attention from this higher perspective.

When we see the beautiful side to all events and experiences we tap the greater understanding that speaks to our inner nature. This in turn, expands its activity and shares its wondrous radiance like a mantle about us. We are here to share, nurture and enjoy beauty like the precious gift it is.

Unconditional love is beauty. Allowing the beauty of our love to unfold is like watching a bud burst forth in its perfect accomplishment as a flower.

Unconditional

Love

Is

Trust

Trust

To learn to trust our self is one of the greatest opportunities and challenges we may ever face. By getting to truly know ourselves, we learn to trust our abilities and act according to our inner truth and light. Without this, we doubt and become suspect to our outer reality. Finding this level of personal awareness and self trust becomes a key quality to our inner peace and harmony.

Each moment we participate with the infinite possibilities and choices of creation. Discerning the highest path through our personal wisdom becomes our training ground. We can accept our creative part in every experience and develop our innate abilities to know and become our potential. With trust, we dare to dream.

Unconditional love is trust. To love ourselves unconditionally is to trust the power of love.

Unconditional

Love

Is

Detachment

Detachment

Loving our creations gives them and us the ability to become more. Naturally, when we hold tightly to anything through fear of loss or attachment, we lose the opportunity to truly experience their precious gifts. Whether people or things, ideas or feelings, we can cherish and enjoy all creation and also release it to expand to a higher expression.

Detachment is the way to experience life to its fullest. When we detach from our need to hold on, we allow the beauty of our reality to unfold and serve us through love. We no longer place limits, opinions, or conditions on the things and people about us. Living in the current moment, we enjoy all expressions just as they are.

Unconditional love is detachment. Loving unconditionally is the ultimate detachment and the ultimate treasure.

Unconditional

Love

Is

Forgiveness

Forgiveness

Forgiveness is the exquisite healer in each of us. To forgive is more than divine - it is a practical and permanent release from our limiting beliefs and perspectives. By letting go of our emotional attachments through forgiveness allows us to love more vibrantly. This is the first step to true inner freedom.

Nothing in life is beyond an act of forgiveness. No matter the perceived pain or grievance, self inflicted or accepted from another, we have the power to forgive. This fantastic gift is ever ready to share the bounty of love through its release into our lives. Before another moment passes, forgive all experiences and people including yourself.

Unconditional love is forgiveness. To love ourselves is to forgive ourselves; to forgive ourselves is to find the pearl within.

Unconditional

Love

Is

New Beginnings

New Beginnings

Every moment of every day is a new beginning. This is the eternal truth of our being. We have the opportunity to change and evolve beyond our current limiting beliefs through the power of our thoughts and feelings. By the mere shift in our attention and attitude, we begin anew and create according to our fresh direction and focus.

If we wish to know who we have been, we can look upon our physical reality now since it reflects our past perspectives. If we want to know who we are becoming, we need to be aware of our thoughts and feelings right now. This moment is the key to all realities past, present, and future as it holds the only opportunity to ever consciously make a change.

Unconditional love is new beginnings. Through the power of self love we find the seed of possibility and a new beginning.

Unconditional Love Is Concentration

Concentration

We can never underestimate the power of our focus and attention. Through our concentration we direct our thoughts and feelings toward the goals and desires we wish to manifest. This is how we make our dreams real and tangible. The accomplishment we seek is correlated to our ability to hold our concentration upon an objective.

When we concentrate our ideas on constructive and loving aspirations, we generate the positive energy to sustain ourselves and our manifestations. Yet, when we allow our attention to drift and sway upon lesser things, we lose our ability to create in the highest way. Thus, we often reap the results of our wayward focus.

Unconditional love is concentration. To concentrate on love is to ensure its ceaseless expression in our lives.

Unconditional

Love

Is

Honesty

Honesty

To intimately know ourselves is to be truly honest with our motivation and intent toward all experiences. Such honesty is born of a love for self and a desire to live in freedom from the shadows of illusionary beliefs. We learn to discern our personal truth from that which we accepted from outer sources.

To honestly, honestly, honestly look at ourselves is to become vulnerable with our deepest nature and touch the greater truth we are. Personal growth and evolution are found through the activity of honest contemplation for inner understanding. The core of our being resides in this purest form of our potential.

Unconditional love is honesty. Through the love of self we learn what life is like to be truly honest and intimate with ourselves and others.

Unconditional
Love
Is
Justice

Justice

When we are just we see through the eyes of our soul and understand the greater picture occurring in each event. Taking a higher view, we decide a course of action based upon truth and intent, not judgment and opinion. In this way, we apply ourselves with unconditional love and expand the possibilities of permanent resolve.

To support ourselves and others through real justice is to know the universe works through free will and personal choice which also reflects our creative responsibility. This fundamental idea reminds us that we all play in the universal game of balancing cause and effect by our individual actions. Once we learn to come from unconditional love, we become beings of cause alone.

Unconditional love is justice. True justice through unconditional love balances the scales and places all energy into harmony.

Unconditional

Love

Is

Integrity

Integrity

There is no mark greater than personal integrity. Beyond each desire and intent to do well in this world, we are ultimately known by our integrity. We must develop this quality with every ounce of our being and apply ourselves to experience its wondrous and loving reflection.

Integrity is found within our every thought, word, deed, and action. When we follow our deepest truth and aspire to greater expression, we pave our path with this loving attribute. Without it, we often founder in a sea of misdeeds, lack of self worth, and loss of self respect. Only through self love and inner honesty can we become the fulfillment of integrity.

Unconditional love is integrity. To be known for your genuine integrity is to be known as a loving person.

Unconditional

Love

Is

Gentleness

Gentleness

When we are gentle in spirit we flow with the natural currents of love and touch all life with this radiance. Having a still and quiet countenance, we emanate the power of self control and mastery over the raging torrents of thoughts and feelings. Love is the guiding force for this gentleness and expresses through the one who comes to know its power.

It takes courage and dedication to apply oneself over the constant desires of the personality. Yet, the results are far more fantastic than the pursuit of a momentary ego pleasure. For when we are gentle, we touch the deeper aspects of our being and allow ourselves to unfold in grace and charm.

Unconditional love is gentleness. Only through a gentle and loving approach to life do we finally experience the sublime essence of what life is really all about.

Unconditional

Love

Is

Youth

Youth

In the innocence of the child we find our true potential. Carefree and filled with imagination, we can explore the farthest reaches of our minds and emotions. We place no blocks or obstacles before us, instead we experience each moment in the peace and perfection intended. As children we hold these natural and simple ideals within our expression.

Each moment is pure and perfect when we step beyond our limiting beliefs and imposed structures acquired in adulthood. We never actually lose our ability to express the fullness of our imagination; we only push it away in search of something outside ourselves. If we stray too far, we forget our original design and the magic begins to fade. Yet, it is never too late to reclaim our youth and once again experience life as it is meant to be.

Unconditional love is youth. Love yourself enough to regain the youthful approach to life that sits quietly inside awaiting your embrace.

Unconditional

Love

Is

Alertness

Alertness

As we awaken from a dreamy sleep, we start to notice our thoughts and feelings and ability to create. Through the gift of imagination and the power of willingness, we have all we require to paint on our canvas of life. The more we cultivate this grand awareness, the more we reap the experiences of our conscious involvement. We become alert and aware of life itself.

It is no longer necessary to be a bystander in life and allow things to happen to us. By being alert to our intuition and quiet wisdom, we can consciously direct the energies about us to manifest our dreams. Staying mindful of our inner prompting and higher desires helps keep us focused upon the goals we seek.

Unconditional love is alertness. Alertness is being aware of the power of love in action, spreading its vibrancy around all of our creations.

Unconditional
Love
Is
Inspiration

Inspiration

Inspiration is the timely awareness of opportunity. With a quiet mind and in a reflective state, we increase our ability to perceive ideas directly from our higher mind and feelings. Capturing these moments of great insight, we can clearly see the solution to any challenges.

Knowing that answers always exist for any problem we face opens the door for inspiring ideas to come forth. Whether for our creative endeavors or daily routines, we have a powerful imagination that can help us develop new ways of doing things. Tapping this vital reservoir is part of an ever expanding journey of greater wisdom and inspiration.

Unconditional love is inspiration. The power of love reveals the highest level of inspiration to us all.

Unconditional

Love

Is

Guidance

Guidance

When we follow our heart, we are engaging our inner guidance and intuition. Such a path never leads us astray. By following this internal direction, we are also the most helpful in assisting others to connect with their own truth and understanding. As we learn to connect with this inner guidance we help guide others to their wisdom. This is our gift to share with the world around us.

Trusting our inner prompting and insights, we find greater flow occurring in every endeavor. Each time we stop to listen deep within, we acknowledge our personal source of wisdom, love, and power. This fantastic guide is always with us as our higher self and knows the next appropriate step for us to take.

Unconditional love is guidance. Love provides the perfect guidance in every experience and assures us of personal growth, compassion, and joy.

Unconditional

Love

Is

Generosity

Generosity

To be generous is to understand the fundamental principle of life: to give is to receive. We now understand we can give much more than material possessions, we give the gift of love through its many beautiful qualities. Sharing our energy this way expands the world around us.

Harmony, peace, laughter, wisdom, and compassion are just a few of the generous expressions we hold within. So are joy and kindness, courage and hope. They are all qualities we can give to ourselves and others. These gifts require no conditions or expectations since they come freely from the heart.

Unconditional love is generosity. To be generous is to know and be the embodiment of unconditional love.

Unconditional

Love

Is

Activity

Activity

Life is an activity and without it we cease to have meaningful purpose. When we seek to express our dreams, we flow with the natural currents of active participation in everything we engage. This leads us to joyful creations in all facets of our daily pursuits.

We take action to accomplish results. From our originating idea to the actual steps that manifest physical things in our reality, we are forever maintaining a focus through our thoughts and feelings. This inner activity and focus is the beginning point of every accomplishment within or without.

Unconditional love is activity. Whenever we actively engage unconditional love, we are setting into motion the most powerful force in the universe.

Unconditional

Love

Is

Understanding

Understanding

To understand who we are allows us to cultivate our inner riches. When we know more about our innate abilities, strengths, and weaknesses, we begin to unfold our potential in a grand way. In the same fashion, we begin to understand those around us and their potential.

True understanding is found from a higher perspective. It requires an unbiased and objective approach to us and others. Without judgment or opinion, we learn to observe our thoughts, feelings, words, deeds, and actions. From this perspective, we notice the things we can correct through loving action and which to release through genuine forgiveness.

Unconditional love is understanding. To understand ourselves through love is to realize the power of life in its greatest expression.

Unconditional

Love

Is

Creativity

Creativity

Everyone has the natural ability to create according to their focus of attention, use of imagination and desire to manifest. We do it every moment of every day. Whether artist or musician, homemaker or business person, each of us uses the same process of creativity in everything we do.

We are forever gathering and using ideas, resources and numerous elements and ingredients in many creative ways to bring together our experiences in life. It does not matter how we may perceive our creative talents, we are applying this vibrant energy each moment as we experience our reality. With a simple change in our perspective, we can know ourselves as the creative beings we are.

Unconditional love is creativity. Naturally creating our life through love is the most profound creation of all.

Unconditional

Love

Is

Imagination

Imagination

The gift of our imagination is the golden key to all possibilities. Beyond all our limiting perceptions and beliefs, we have the incredible power to imagine infinite numbers of new realities. The opportunities are boundless and the dreams expansive when we focus within and use this innate genius held within our consciousness.

Like the springtime planting of a garden, we must cultivate and nurture this wondrous faculty of imagination. Only in this way will we ever know our potential and trust in our ability to conceive new ideas. With our imagination we can mold and fashion any possibility into its highest expression before experiencing it in the outer world.

Unconditional love is imagination. If we can dream it we can build it, and if we use love in the process, there is no limit to the achievements we can reach.

Unconditional

Love

Is

Happiness

Happiness

Happiness is a state of being that has at its core a sense of self love and acceptance. Being at peace with the process of life is the starting point to generating a happy perspective. As we express more of this quality we experience a profusion of it in our life. Happiness is an expansive quality that touches and transforms everyone and everything with its innate joyous nature.

What else is there than to be happy under all circumstances? It is as simple as focusing our attention upon the possibility and there we will find happiness waiting for us. When the illusion of discontent tries to interfere, simply turn within and you will touch the giggling heart of an enchanted self.

Unconditional love is happiness. Ultimate happiness is found in loving ourselves and everyone else unconditionally while knowing all is well and always will be.

Unconditional

Love

Is

Purpose

Purpose

Each of us has a special gift to share with the rest of humanity - it is the gift of love. With such a noble purpose, it is easy to see the beauty and wonder of life upon this planet. By simply being ourselves and focusing our attention on love, we fulfill our destiny every moment.

Many maintain an ongoing external search for meaning and purpose, yet all the while we are only a thought away from the truth of our existence. The qualities of love reside within and simply await our conscious use. As we accept and become these higher positive thoughts and feelings, we lift everything and everyone around us.

Unconditional love is purpose. To express the power of unconditional love is to know and experience our purpose in life.

Unconditional Love Is Mastery

Mastery

We pave the road to self mastery by the steps of self correction. This exceptional journey of learning and evolving allows us to consciously use life's universal energy to understand our creative ability. When we come from love we experience our highest potential. However, when we allow negativity to enter our world we constrict our boundless possibilities.

Mastery is the art of holding our attention upon our greatest ideals. It also includes radiating unconditional love to all facets of life. Mastery places our higher wisdom in charge of our outer personality and ego. Taking one step at a time, we learn to harness this incredible energy and channel it for its utmost loving effect.

Unconditional love is mastery. Whenever we come from the power of love, we master the moment and express our limitless potential.

Unconditional Love Is Grace

Grace

To come from a state of grace is the embodiment of unconditional love. This exquisite energy transforms even the hardest experiences, melting away the discord and revealing the love within. Each time we choose to stand in the light of grace, we empower our reality with this fantastic quality.

Graceful and serene, we can walk amongst the chaos of destructive appearances and remain untouched. In turn, we act as a beacon of comfort to those around us. This calm state knows the power of love that ever dwells within.

Unconditional love is grace. Beautiful beyond measure, the experience of grace is an astounding quality of love.

Unconditional

Love

Is

Abundance

Abundance

There are billions of stars in our galaxy alone and infinite grains of sand upon a single shore. This is an abundant universe in every respect. As creative beings, we have the limitless capacity to unfold our potential in the same way. When properly understood through love, there is more than enough to fulfill every person's dreams and fondest desires.

We have all we require to sustain our basic needs and more. As we learn to use the universal energy of life in its highest form, we find a boundless supply ever waiting to express itself through love. Seek to the stars and remember your heritage as an infinite creative being.

Unconditional love is abundance. Unconditional love is an unlimited and abundant way of being.

Unconditional

Love

Is

Strength

Strength

Strength is a quality that reflects our inner trust in self. When we know ourselves, we know we are here to utilize our energy to bring good in life. It is a personal vitality and acceptance of our potential. Believing in ourselves, we become stronger in every way.

We must have courage to go beyond our perceived limits. This is never a measure of brawn or physical accomplishments. Instead, we experience it through realizing our dreams and loving our world without condition. It takes true strength and courage to live one's truth and embody our higher ideals.

Unconditional love is strength. Seek the limitless power within and share this strength with all the love of your being.

Unconditional
Love
Is
Sincerity

Sincerity

As we cultivate and unfold our loving self we naturally become more sincere. Our inner wisdom guides the way to expressing this higher quality. With sincerity comes a sense of integrity in all we do or say. Expressing through love insures we are ever modeling this wonderful attribute.

Sincerity is simply being natural in our thoughts, feelings, and actions. We rise above the personality perceptions and limitations and choose to be ourselves. We own our truth and allow ourselves to express the positive possibilities each moment.

Unconditional love is sincerity. It is easy to be sincere when we come from unconditional love.

Unconditional

Love

Is

Courage

Courage

Courage is one of the greatest qualities we can ever develop. We need to have courage to see our dreams become a reality and to overcome the obstacles along the way. It helps us find the strength and determination we often believe we do not have. This is the value of cultivating the incredible resource of courage.

When we encounter appearances and circumstances that seem the most challenging to us, we use our courage to dig deep within ourselves and find the power to rise above any situation. Incorporating the power of love ensures us of our victory in the process. This is the how we come to know and comprehend our real potential and inner character.

Unconditional love is courage. When we embrace our courage, we love ourselves and carry trust and compassion in our hearts.

Unconditional Love Is Choice

Choice

Within each thought is the possibility to choose what we wish to create and with each feeling is the power to manifest our desires. Our reality is merely a reflection of these choices. Whether conscious of this process or not, we hold the power to create and direct our potential in each moment. It is our choice.

Choice is the ultimate freedom we each share. When we come from love, we encourage the highest choices. By focusing our attention upon this fantastic inner awareness, we learn to discern between the many possibilities and decide which we want to ultimately experience. This infinite universal power simply awaits our acknowledgement and use.

Unconditional love is choice. The more we choose to love in each moment, the more we experience love in our life.

Unconditional

Love

Is

Confidence

Confidence

The inner self is the true guide to our possibilities and potential. Turning within, we learn to trust our abilities, strength and wisdom and find the confidence to move forward. Without confidence, we are destined to founder in a sea of mistrust and low self esteem. It is up to us to unfold the beauty of trusting ourselves.

We can only experience confidence within and must make conscious choices to find out what we are truly capable of. This builds the character of personal fortitude and assures us of our worth. Taking one step at a time, we lay our foundation by believing and relying in ourselves.

Unconditional love is confidence. When we love ourselves unconditionally, we find all the confidence we could ever desire.

Unconditional

Love

Is

Health

Health

True health is found in positive thoughts and emotions. Knowing that our body always seeks balance, reminds us that health is our natural expression. Focusing our attention on loving thoughts and feelings insures our radiant perfection and vitality.

When we experience dis-ease with life, we are really allowing our inner reality to waver with negativity and limitation. The mere shifting of our perspectives makes the difference in how our body responds. When we remain in harmony and keep our attention upon higher and more positive thoughts and feelings, we maintain our mental, emotional, and physical balance.

Unconditional love is health. Health is a state of being that comes from loving unconditionally.

Unconditional

Love

Is

Unity

Unity

We all live upon this wonderful planet sharing our laughter and tears, hopes and dreams. It matters not what size, shape, color or creed, our fundamental foundation is in our collective human experience and potential to become more. Unity recognizes the oneness of humanity and the possibilities to create together through love.

Whenever we separate ourselves through judging ourselves or another, we limit our experience. Through limited awareness, opinions, and criticism, we deny the fullness of each other's potential. The reverse is also true, when we come from love and unity we help ourselves and our fellow travelers become all we can be.

Unconditional love is unity. Loving everyone unconditionally insures we can live in unity and peace in this world, when we choose to do so.

Unconditional

Love

Is

Vitality

Vitality

When we feel alive and centered, we emanate an aura of vitality. This vibrant energy radiates to those around us and often inspires others to become more. By simply living in balance and pursuing our loving potential, we naturally generate this exceptional quality of love.

Our positive attitude lifts every activity we engage in and every person we encounter. With minimal effort to maintain harmony and joy in all we do, feel, and think, we keep our world in balance. This reflects back to us through our happy interactions and experiences with others.

Unconditional love is vitality. When we come from love, we live our lives with the vitality only such unlimited energy can ever provide.

Unconditional

Love

Is

Power

Power

Power by itself is little more than energy unleashed. Yet, when coupled with love and wisdom, it creates a triune activity transforming all it touches. Using unconditional love as our intention releases an infinite power of beauty and perfection. It is a sustaining and permanent action dissolving all discord.

As external power gives way to internal power, we learn to master and focus the love we have within. This is bringing a new dawn of conscious awareness in our world. As we grow and change through the power of love, we are becoming our infinite potential.

Unconditional love is power. Love is energy with power of the greatest magnitude.

Unconditional

Love

Is

Serenity

Serenity

Peace begins within and when we build a foundation of this activity we develop a sense of serenity. Each time we turn inward, we compel our attention to rest upon higher ideals. Calmness, harmony, and quiet joy are true indicators of this gentle self. It is a simple choice how we wish to experience life.

By letting go of fears and doubts, we stand in our natural power. Even in the midst of chaos we can retain our composure and know the strength of our love. This is the potential we wield every moment when we consciously choose it. Like the delicate morning sun, we stand serene and bless all life.

Unconditional love is serenity. Peace and serenity come from one who knows the power they share from their loving heart.

Unconditional

Love

Is

Courtesy

Courtesy

The world around us is part of our creation and we are an integral part of every person, place, and condition. Naturally, the energies we give out must affect us in the same way. A simple act of courtesy allows us to share the love, joy, and forgiveness we have within. We acknowledge our part in this grand play that benefits everyone.

Kindness comes from a generous heart and a trusting spirit. When we release the need to hold anger, hate, or criticism, we shift our perspective to the higher expressions. We begin by extending courtesy to ourselves, recognizing our personal dreams and potential and then radiate this quality to the rest of our reality.

Unconditional love is courtesy. This delightful planet grants us the courtesy to enjoy her bounty, it is time we share this love in return.

Unconditional
Love
Is
Success

Success

We can never measure success by the things we acquire. Instead, it is indicated by the love we learn to generate and provide to those around us. In each act of unconditional love, we show the universe our willingness to live in harmony with all aspects of life. This type of success takes strength and courage that only comes from love.

All material things come and go. Yet, the love we share is a permanent record of our ability to cultivate and use this fantastic energy. Every moment provides us with the opportunity to become a little more loving to ourselves and each other. This undeniable expression leaves us with a heart filled with joy.

Unconditional love is success. Loving unconditionally is the true mark of sustaining success.

Unconditional

Love

Is

Persistence

Persistence

A dream made manifest occurs when we are persistent with our goals. From the initial thought, to the motivation of our feelings, each step unfolds the journey to its completion. Adding love insures our creations are perfect for all concerned. We literally bring our imagination to life.

Persistence is the only way we bring the good things to our world. There is a natural rhythm that builds as we move forward from one activity to the next. Staying with our innermost and heartfelt desires is where our authentic power lies. Realizing and perfecting these dreams gives meaning to our lives.

Unconditional love is persistence. Persistently loving ourselves and each other is the most beautiful dream we can ever manifest.

Unconditional

Love

Is

Achievement

Achievement

Love is the greatest achievement and victory we can ever aspire to. Seeking no limits or conditions, we can graciously choose to love unconditionally each moment. This way we leave a trail of loving expressions behind us and automatically create a future destined for more love. Achieving love in this moment is the most majestic accomplishment.

The outer affairs of our daily life contain many remarkable events. We find strength, courage, and a deep sense of self in many of these achievements. Yet, peace and plenty come from knowing the well-spring of all future achievement resides within. Never needing to turn to the outer for accolades, we naturally live and convey the understanding of love.

Unconditional love is achievement. Reaching for the stars, we find the truest light is in the achievement of unconditional love.

Unconditional

Love

Is

Humility

Humility

To be whole and secure in oneself is to convey an innate humbleness. When we realize others are equals upon the path of life, we also recognize the same infinite potential in each to create. This leads to humility and the understanding that life grants us the opportunity to exist and the dignity of self expression.

To be humble is to acknowledge our inner strength and the innate rights of everyone. Judgment, perceived class or status, or any other limiting idea that separates us does not embody the oneness of life. The forces of the universe keep the equation in balance and show us that we all share in the equality of life. Be gracious with each experience for it leads us onward in our evolving journey.

Unconditional love is humility. The power of love unfolds the petals of the rose with the same humility as the evolving human being.

Unconditional

Love

Is

Energy

Energy

In all of creation there is nothing more vital and exquisite than the energy of unconditional love. At the core of all things is the frequency of love, the highest of all vibrations. This energy of love permeates every level and dimension of our reality and sustains the life in each expression. It lifts, raises and connects everything in a positive and dynamic fashion.

Since we naturally find love in all things, we need only look to ourselves to find the love we crave and desire. As we unfold it within our being we automatically begin to radiate more of it to the world about us. Shifting our perspective from doubt and fear to love is the first step in realizing this infinite energizing power.

Unconditional love is energy. All the energy we ever require dwells within the love we hold in our heart.

Unconditional

Love

Is

Ability

Ability

Life sustains us through love. To know the power of love is to realize we have the ability to create all the things we desire. Paying attention to this wondrous guiding force places us upon a fantastic journey. When we follow our innermost dreams and unfold our potential, we sing with life itself. Each moment is a pleasure to be alive.

We are capable of so much and yet deny this power with every negative and critical thought. Every time we choose to think and feel negatively, we empower this draining energy. This can draw us away from our potential and keep us mired in limitation. Only through the power of love can we reclaim our attention and pursue our destiny.

Unconditional love is ability. Love without limitation is the most potent and capable energy we can ever engage.

Unconditional

Love

Is

Respect

Respect

A major step to loving unconditionally is the understanding of respect. Each of us has the free will to create life as we choose. Naturally, if we wish to experience freedom, we must give freedom first. This includes giving ourselves the freedom to pursue our personal dreams and aspirations. The only condition life requires of us is to not impose our will upon another.

Respect is the simple act of allowing and honoring one another to express their diversity and infinite potential. When we come from our heart, all things come into natural balance and order. If we see through limited perspectives, we often imply that others infringe upon our space and creation. Only through love do we find the remedy to this misguided perception.

Unconditional love is respect. Respect and love one another without condition or limit.

Unconditional
Love
Is
Potential

Potential

Loving constantly and unconditionally is our greatest potential. This limitless energy knows no bounds and fills us with unlimited imagination to create anew. As we embrace and use this energy, it automatically replenishes and sustains us in every activity. Nothing in life is more potent than coming from love.

Recognizing the power within our heart teaches us of the same potential in others. When we bring this regal energy into our expression, we become a beacon of light to all those around us. The most magnificent gift we can bestow upon others is that all things are indeed possible through love.

Unconditional love is potential. Become your exquisite potential through the power of your unconditional love.

About the Author

Harold W. Becker has dedicated his life to understanding, living and sharing unconditional love. In 1990 he formed his consulting company, Internal Insights, and in 2000 he founded the non-profit, The Love Foundation, Inc., with the mission of "Inspiring people to love unconditionally."

In his desire to touch the world with this timeless message of love, Harold conceived Global Love Day, an international celebration of humanity, held annually each May 1st.

He is the author of several additional books including, *Internal Power: Seven Doorways to Self Discovery*, *Unconditional Love – An Unlimited Way of Being* and *Inspiring Unconditional Love – Reflections from the Heart* and wrote and hosted his own PBS special program entitled, *Unconditional Love – A Guide to Personal Freedom* available on DVD.

Harold has an MBA and enjoys bringing his inspirational and motivational vision into every facet of his life including his business activities, writing, speaking, seminars and consulting. Blending incredible insight and intuition with humor, compassion and kindness, he encourages people to love unconditionally.

You can reach Harold through the following web sites:
www.internalinsights.com
www.thelovefoundation.com
www.globalloveday.com
www.whitefirepublishing.com